GAIL GIBBONS

MY BASKETBALL BOOK

HarperCollins**Publishers**

Special thanks to Fawn Carter,
physical education instructor, Waits River
Valley School, Corinth, Vermont

My Basketball Book
Copyright © 2000 by Gail Gibbons
Printed in Singapore at Tien Wah Press.
All rights reserved.
www.harperchildrens.com

Library of Congress Cataloging-in-Publication Data
Gibbons, Gail.
My basketball book / Gail Gibbons.
p. cm.
ISBN 0-688-17140-0
1. Basketball—Juvenile literature. I. Title. GV885.1.G52 2000
99-87902

10 9 8 7 6 5 4 3
❖

Basketball is fun, whether you are playing yourself or rooting for your favorite team.

SNEAKERS with
rubber soles

BASKETBALL

To play, you need a basketball, a basket . . .

BASKET

and sometimes a uniform.

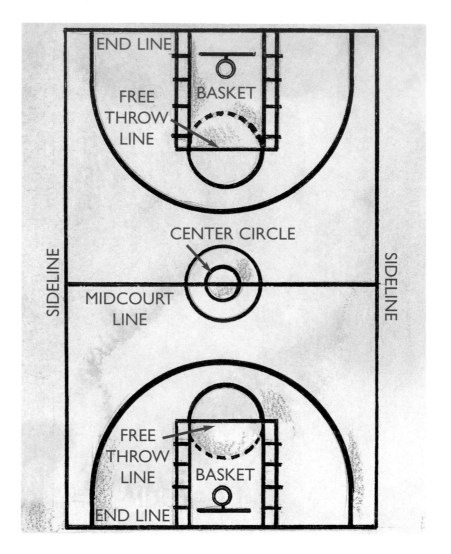

Basketball is usually played indoors on a smooth wooden basketball court.

There are usually five players on a team. The members of each team work together to score the most points. To score points, the ball must go through the other team's basket.

FORWARD

GUARDS are usually small and fast. They move the ball down-court to the other team's basket.

GUARD

Each team has two guards, two forwards, and one center.

FORWARD

Each player has a position to play, but he or she can go anywhere on the court. The players move the ball by bouncing it with one hand, called dribbling, or by passing it to a teammate.

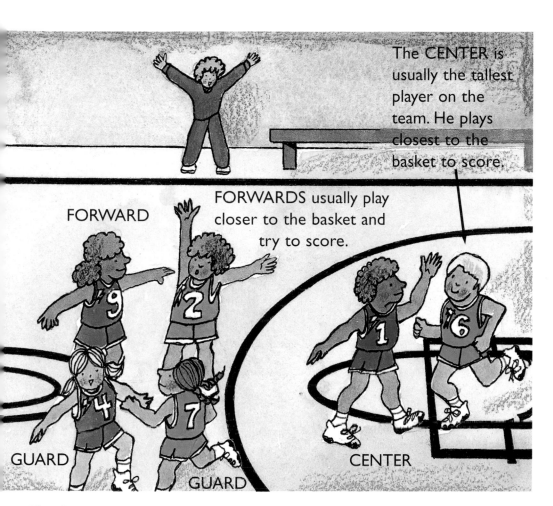

The CENTER is usually the tallest player on the team. He plays closest to the basket to score.

FORWARD

FORWARDS usually play closer to the basket and try to score.

GUARD

GUARD

CENTER

Each player must guard a player from the other team. The team on offense has the ball. The team on defense tries to stop the other team from scoring.

Games are often made up of four twelve-minute quarters. Basketball games for kids are usually shorter.

The COACH guides his or her team.

The REFEREE makes sure the game is played fairly.

COACH

Let's play basketball! The referee tosses the ball up in the air between two players. Each tries to tap the ball to one of their teammates.

The Comets, on offense, move the ball toward the Blasters' basket. One player dribbles closer and closer.

The Blaster defense is working hard to keep the player from scoring. Then there's a quick pass . . .

A successful throw is called a FIELD GOAL.

and the center grabs the ball. With a leap, he shoots the ball into the basket. Two points for the Comets!

Now it's the Blasters' turn. The ball is thrown-in from behind the end line. As the ball is moved down the court, a Comet guard steals it and runs to make another basket.

The score is 4 to 0, Comets.

ME
OD VISITORS
12   14

TIME CLOCK

The referee blows a whistle to signal a foul or other violation to stop the TIME CLOCK. When the game begins again, the clock restarts.

Players must follow a set of rules. If a player takes more than a certain number of steps while holding the ball, it's called traveling. The ball then goes to the other team. Also, a player cannot go out-of-bounds.

When a player is fouled while shooting a basket, he or she gets two free throws.

If a player is tripped or pushed, that's a foul, and the player gets a free throw from the free throw line. A free throw that goes in the basket counts as one point.

Each team gets a certain number of time-outs.

When a coach wants to talk to her team, she calls for a time-out. Play stops, and both teams go back to their benches.

Every player gets a chance to dribble, pass, or steal the ball. It's exciting to help make a basket. Finally, the buzzer sounds. It's halftime, and the players catch their breaths.

A REBOUND happens when the ball doesn't go into the basket and the other team takes the ball away. Rebounding is often the center's job.

After halftime, the teams switch sides. The players run up and down the court. The Comet center snatches a rebound and moves the ball toward the Blasters' basket.

It's a basket! By the bottom of the fourth quarter, the Comets are winning 49 to 48.

The time clock keeps ticking. There are only twenty-four seconds left in the game. One last wild shot . . .

and it goes through the basket! The final score is 50 to 49—a win for the Blasters. Everyone cheers. It's been such a good game.

MY BASKETBALL GLOSSARY

 assist: a pass to a teammate who scores

 backcourt: the half of the court that a team is defending

 basket: the name for a score during play

 defense: working to prevent baskets, by blocking shots, stealing the ball, and other means

 dunk: slamming the ball into the basket from above the level of the rim

 field goal: a basket that is made during play

 frontcourt: the half of a court that a team is attacking

 jump ball: used to start or restart play

 offense: working to score baskets, by taking shots, passing the ball, and other means

 sportsmanship: playing fairly and enjoying a game, no matter who wins or loses

 teamwork: playing together as a team, encouraging and supporting all of your teammates

 throw-in: a way to restart play when a ball has gone out-of-bounds or after the referee has stopped play

 turnover: when a team loses the ball without having made a shot